ABOUT DYING

In Memory of Charles P. Balsam

First published in the United States of America
in 1974 by the Walker Publishing Company, Inc.

Published simultaneously in Canada by Fitzhenry &
Whiteside, Limited, Toronto.

ISBN: 0-8027-6172-0

Library of Congress Catalog Card Number: 73-15268

Printed in the United States of America.

ABOUT DYING

An Open Family Book For Parents And Children Together

by Sara Bonnett Stein

in cooperation with
Gilbert W. Kliman, M.D.
Director

Doris Ronald
Educational Director,
The Cornerstone Nursery-Kindergarten

Ann S. Kliman
Director,
Situational Crisis Service

Phyllis Schwartz
Community Coordinator

The Center for Preventive
Psychiatry
White Plains, New York

photography by Dick Frank
graphic design, Michel Goldberg

Walker and Company
New York, New York
Created by Media Projects Incorporated

A Note About This Book

When your child was a baby, you took him to the doctor to have him immunized for childhood illnesses. The injections hurt a little, but you knew they would prepare his body to cope with far more serious threats in the future. Yet there are other threats as painful and destructive to a child's growth as physical illness: Separation from his parents, a death in the family, a new baby, fears and fantasies of his own imagining that hurt as much as pain itself. These Open Family Books are to help adults prepare children for common hurts of childhood.

Caring adults try to protect their child from difficult events. But still that child has ears that overhear, eyes that read the faces of adults around him. If people are sad, he knows it. If people are worried, he knows it. If people are angry, he knows that too.

What he doesn't know—if no one tells him—is the whole story. In his attempts to make sense of what is going on around him, he fills in the fragments he has noticed with fantasied explanations of his own which, because he is a child, are often more frightening than the truth.

We protect children because we know them to be different, more easily damaged than ourselves. But the difference we sense is not widely understood. Children are more easily damaged because they cannot make distinctions yet between what is real and what is unreal, what is magic and what is logic. The tiger under a child's bed at night is as real to him as the tiger in the zoo. When he wishes a bad thing, he believes his wish can make the bad thing happen. His fearful imagining about what is going on grips him because he has no way to test the truth of it.

It is the job of parents to support and explain reality, to guide a child toward the truth even if it is painful. The dose may be small, just as a dose of vaccine is adjusted to the smallness of a baby; but even if it is a little at a time, it is only straightforwardness that gives children the internal strength to deal with things not as they imagine them to be, but as they are.

To do that, parents need to understand what sorts of fears, fantasies, misunderstandings are common to early childhood—what they might expect at three years old, or at five, or seven. They need simpler ways to explain the way

complicated things are. The adult text of each of these
books, in the left hand column, explains extraordinary
ways that ordinary children between three and eight years
old attempt to make sense of difficult events in their lives.
It puts in words uncomplicated ways to say things. It is
probably best to read the adult text several times before
you read the book to your child, so you will get a comfort-
able feel for the ideas and so you won't be distracted as you
talk together. If your child can read, he may one day
be curious to read the adult text. That's all right. What's
written there is the same as what you are talking about
together. The pictures and the words in large print are to
start the talking between you and your child. The stories
are intense enough to arouse curiosity and feeling. But they
are reasonable, forthright and gentle, so a child can deal
with the material at whatever level he is ready for.

The themes in these Open Family Books are common to
children's play. That is no accident. Play, joyous but also
serious, is the way a child enacts himself a little bit at a
time, to get used to events, thoughts and feelings he is
confused about. Helping a child keep clear on the difference
between what is real and what is fantasy will not restrict
a child's creativity in play. It will let him use fantasy more
freely because it is less frightening.

In some ways, these books won't work. No matter how a
parent explains things, a child will misunderstand some
part of the explanation, sometimes right away, sometimes
in retrospect, weeks or even months later. Parents really
can't help this fact of psychological life. Nothing in human
growing works all at once, completely or forever. But
parents can keep the channels of communication open so
that gradually their growing child can bring his version of
the way things are closer to the reality. Each time you
read an Open Family Book and talk about it together, your
child will take in what at that moment is most useful to
him. Another day, another month, years later, other aspects
of the book will be useful to him in quite different ways.
The book will not have changed; what he needs, what he
notices, how he uses it will change.

But that is what these books are for: To open between adult
and child the potential for growth that exists in human
beings of all ages.

This was Snow.

There is a look of innocence to childhood—a white bird, sweet faces, a sense of no tomorrow. But there is a tomorrow. One of every twenty children will face the death of a parent during childhood. Virtually every child will experience the death of a pet, a neighbor, a friend, a grandparent. How he is helped to deal with dying as it happens in his everyday world will ready your son or daughter even for a death that is crucial in his life.

This book is about everyday dying, the kind your child, every child, meets early in his own life—the kind he must learn to mourn.

He was alive.
He could fly.
Jane and Eric
could hold him
in their hands.
So they
loved him.

Mourning is not just feeling sad. It is the specific psychological process by which human beings become able to give up some of the feelings they have invested in a person who no longer exists, and extend their love to the living. Mourning is hard, emotional work. It is pulling memories into focus, and allowing ourselves to be touched by the feelings they carry with them. It is struggling with guilt that we might have done better and anger that we are left alone. It is taking up the disrupted threads of our life and finding new patterns to weave of them. It is giving up a person who is no more.

But this is just the problem children have. While they are little, they don't believe a life can cease to exist. They don't know much about time; they don't understand "forever." They think dying is reversible and the dead can come back to life. Until they are quite sure a person is no more, and will never be, they cannot finish the work of mourning. And if they cannot finish it, they cannot free themselves to go on with life and love and growing. Only through adult honesty and support can a small child work through death in ways that help him to grow.

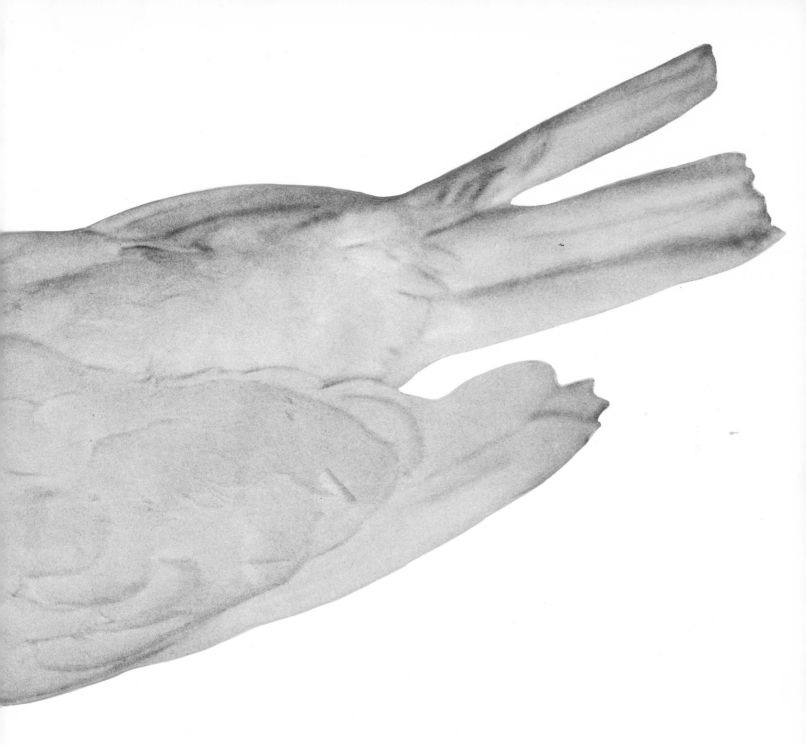

One day he was dead.

Honesty and support start here, with a small dead bird. Yes, Snow is dead. Yes, we are sad. No, he will not move, he will not be warm, he will not ever be alive again.

It may feel neither easy nor natural to say the truth. We fear death; we are used to avoiding it. Old people are taken out of our sight to die. We keep silent about what is really happening. Dead goldfish are flushed down toilets, dead hamsters dumped in garbage pails so a child can't see, won't know the truth. Yet some small animal may become your child's first introduction to death. Don't make it a whispered word. Death happens.

His head felt too loose. His body was stiff. He was cold. He didn't move anymore. He was dead.

Years after a pet bird was buried, one child told his mother: I wanted to keep him because I could hold him in my hand when he was dead; there was something important to find out.

Children are curious about dead things because they need to know what dead is really like. Handling a dead animal is like investigating the insides of a clockwork toy: It is a way to sort out the real from the imagined. It may be hard to speak to children of rotting and of bones. But there is no way around it. Dead bodies get smelly, and rot until only bones are left. That is why dead animals, dead people, are buried or cremated.

Eric felt like keeping Snow. He was interested in dead animals. Mommy said he would smell awful. They would have to bury him.

It is a carefulness of our own feelings that chooses—even for a bird—a pretty box, a soft handkerchief, a protected spot for his grave. When a mother helps to find just the right box, when a father gives up his good handkerchief, it is a way of saying how important children's feelings are, how shared, how human, how good to express to one another.

The neighbors' children didn't even know Snow, but any life that has died has to do with them. It will be a lovely burial; they will talk about it afterwards just like grownups talk about a beautiful funeral.

Jane found a box. Eric wrapped Snow in Daddy's soft handkerchief. Their brother Michael came to see. Their friends came to see too.

What does your child think will happen to the bird after it is buried? Not yet sure what dying is, he might think the bird will get cold, or lonely, feel scared of the dark or hungry for his dinner. He may worry whether he can still breathe under the dirt. The truth must be said again and again: The dead bird no longer thinks or sees or moves or feels. It is only the children who are alive who will feel lonely for the bird they loved.

They dug a hole.
They put the box in it.
They covered it with dirt.
They put a red flower on the grave.

It is not by accident that we say before the grave, "Dust thou art, and unto dust shalt thou return." Or that we plant into that dust new things to grow. It is a way we put a single life into proportion with Life itself—a continuous freshening, persistently springing from dead leaves, bare graves. The words of human burial are good words for birds and beetles and pet mice. The living flowers that mark a human grave are good markers for little animals too.

The bird was dead,
but the flower was alive.

Remembering builds clear boundaries for people. Memories are of when the bird was living. Now the bird is dead. And the closeness of remembering together helps children put words to thoughts so parents can learn from them what's confused, misunderstood and scary. Eric thought germs killed the bird, and worried that germs are catching. Jane feared the bird had died because she once forgot to feed him.

Little children have no way to untangle these mistaken ideas by themselves. Parents can only help them if they know what the ideas are.

"Do you remember how you held Snow in your hands and could pat him," said Mommy.

"I remember when we got Snow. Grandpa gave him to us," said Eric.

This was Grandpa,
who gave
the children Snow;
who drew pictures
with them,
and smiled;
who took them
to the park.

Worried faces and whispers say it: Something is very wrong. Life does not go on as usual. The everyday of suppertimes, of daily errands, old jokes, warm cuddles that enfold a child within his family is suddenly hurried meals, baby sitters, phone calls, serious conversations that push the child out. He notices, he overhears—he knows.

It is best to say what's wrong and not make of dying a lonely child's guessing game. You can explain that the person is very very seriously sick. You can say that a person could die of that sickness. And if you can, help your child visit like this child is visiting his grandfather. It is the beginning of saying goodbye for both of them.

Until he got sick. Then the grownups said:

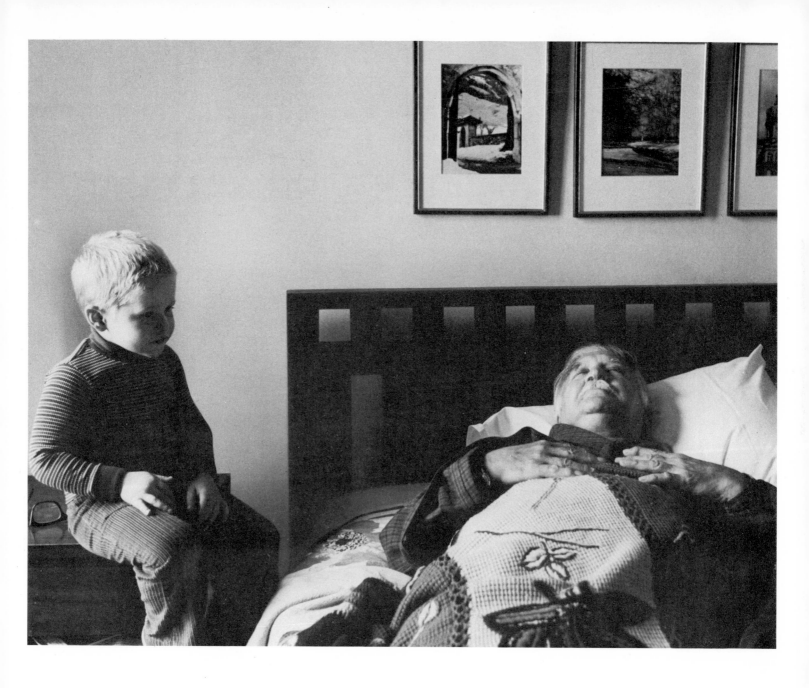

"Be quiet. Grandpa is sick."

Children want to know: Why did he die? If their question is not answered, they will answer it for themselves in ways that are confused and frightening. What if the children had been noisy, had bothered Grandfather? To many young children, that is reason enough for him to die, reason enough to think it is their fault. Even a bad thought in a moment of anger—I hope you die, I wish you were dead—seems to children strong enough to kill. They need to know real reasons, so they know it is not their fault. A simple explanation is appropriate: He had a serious illness. She was old. His head was badly hurt when his car slipped on the road.

Sometimes adults can't bring themselves right away to explain anything to the child. If that is so, tell your child how you feel; let him see your crying. Reassure him that you will talk with him about what happened as soon as you feel able.

Grandpa died. Mommy was crying.

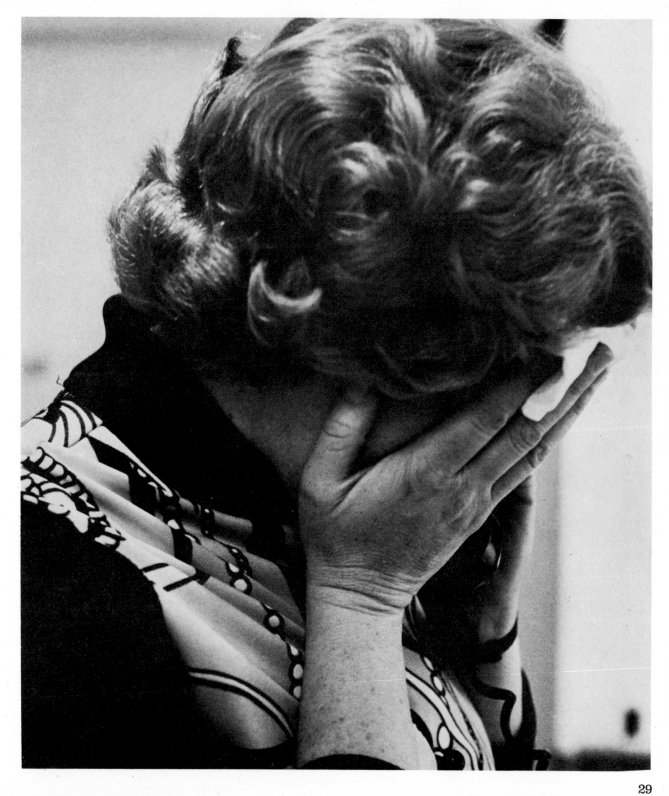

Before the children could part with their dead bird, they held him in their hands to literally grasp the fact of his death. Many children want to see the body of someone they have loved because, to them, seeing is believing. If this is something that is all right with you, your clergyman might help you to explain to others that a child could find it easier to say goodbye to a body than to say goodbye to a box.

If this is something you could not bear, tell your child about your feelings, and listen to his too. People can act differently but still both be sad not to have Grandpa any more.

Like the dead bird, he was put in a box. It was called a coffin. Eric wondered what he looked like now. He wanted to keep the coffin, with Grandpa in it.

It is hard for children to behave the way adults expect at a funeral. They may be somber and silent for a moment, then talk, roam around, laugh and play. That is the nature of children. They can't be still for long. Their feelings, however strong, come out in bursts and seem to vanish. Yet if a child is not allowed to share in the funeral—if he is left to a sandwich and a sitter —it is like saying death is not important in the child's life, it has nothing to do with him. Or it is a secret, too dangerous for him to know about. Or he cannot share with other people in his life the feelings that they feel. It is kindness to think of children as caring, as human. They too must take leave of those they knew in life. Even if a child stays at a funeral for five minutes, it is long enough to say goodbye.

They went to Grandpa's funeral, and to the graveyard.

People shy from using the word dead with children. But the words that may sound better are worse. Since a child can see that something sad and awful has really happened, words like gone away or asleep can make the everyday events of life—leaving for a vacation, going to bed at night—seem dangerous. Some words of religious imagery have pitfalls too. To an adult rocks are real in a different way than words are real, or a belief, or an image. But to a child everything is real in the same way. Heaven is a place above the clouds. An angel is a person who has grown wings, who flies, alive in the sky. If Grandfather is "watching over you," he must see the bad things you do.

The ways a child may interpret what is said to him can interfere with his mourning: He may think the person is not really dead after all, but only "gone to Heaven;" and he could think the person is still able to direct his behavior, like a punishing conscience.

Parents have to help their child think more abstractly, more like they do. If they believe in a hereafter, they might explain that Grandpa's soul, his spirit, is like our memory of him—it can't be touched, but it can't be destroyed either.

At the graveyard the coffin was put
in the earth, and covered with dirt.
They had to leave Grandpa there.

The stories of these children are true stories. They are about healthy children reacting to the death of a much-loved grandparent in normal ways. But what is normal to children often seems inappropriate, even callous, to adults, as though children feel neither as strongly nor as deeply as they. What we do not realize is that it is not feelings that are lacking, but the child's ability to defend himself against the pain of sadness and loss. What looks like lack of feeling is often a child's attempt to shield himself in his own way against too much feeling at once.

It is too much for Michael to lose all of Grandpa at once. He grabs on to whatever he can of him. He feels empty inside and tries to fill his emptiness with food. Eating greedily and looting possessions are two ordinary ways children try to fill the void in their lives. This can be explained to the child. It can be explained to shocked adults too.

Then Michael took a lot of Grandpa's things and ate all his cookies too. But he still felt empty inside.

Why might a child act so naughty, just now, when everyone is sad? A child might be angry at Grandfather for leaving her like that. Since grownups appear able to do anything they wish—have what they want, do what they like, go where they please—it seems to children within an adult's power to not die. Jane at six is old enough to feel abandoned by Grandpa, betrayed and angry. It is hard on the family to find, just when they have little energy to cope with more troubles, patience to deal with an irritable and irritating child who doesn't even act sad.

But the tears come—at unexpected times, for what seems no reason at all. The big loss hurts too much, so Jane cries for little things, for trivial matters. Her mother says, "I see how sad you are. You must miss Grandpa very much."

Jane was mad at Grandpa for dying. She teased and tore things up. Then she cried and cried and cried.

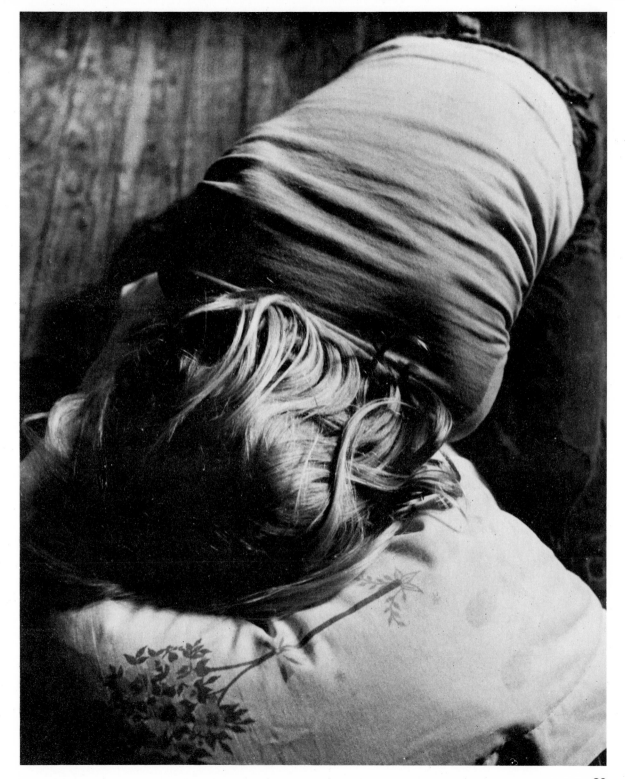

Many children play of dying. "Bang, bang, you're dead" is not a onetime thing, but a childhood theme played out in many forms for many years. They play to test the realness of an idea and to become aware, in small doses, of how they feel about it. Jane is playing out an old idea of hers, one she has almost grown out of. She lovingly holds to the thought that dead people, dead bugs, might become alive again. But the bugs never drink the water, never eat the food. Little by little, Jane will give up a hope that Grandpa is not really dead.

Jane played making graves for dead bugs. She made beds for them to sleep in; she filled little shells with water and food. She wished the bugs would be alive, and eat and see and move. But she knew they were dead.

One day
it was raining.
Eric said:
"Why do only men
have black umbrellas?"
People wore black
clothes when
Grandpa died.
Black made Eric
worry about dying.

Grandpa was a man. Grandpa died. Black clothes were death clothes. Eric thought: Black umbrellas mean that men die. Couldn't little boys die too? His mother explains that sometimes children die, but only of a very serious sickness or a very bad accident. Almost every child lives a long, long time, until he is old. Everyone has to die when they get old. Eric says, "Are you old? Could you die?" "I could," says his mother, "but I take very good care of myself—I use my seat belt and get my checkup so that I probably won't die until long after you are a grown man."

People are born. They grow to be children and then adults. They get old, they die. It is helpful for children to know that dying is the final part of everyone's life, not a thing that happens only to some people.

Children do not want something at such a time for no reason. Anything they do—all of what they do —has meaning. We can't always understand what burying beetles or buying umbrellas means to a child. But perhaps, not always understanding, it is best to bend to little things, knowing they may be more important than we know.

He asked: "Mommy, can I have a red umbrella?" The red umbrella made him feel safe.

The things we did together, the things we said, the good times and the bad times, the funny stories, special presents, holiday doings, daily ways, and all the places we went with one another—these are ours for all our years. But if a child must remember all by himself, his mind might trick him in some ways, thinking of the rain and not the sun. A family can trade all kinds of memories together, pulling out snapshots, laughing over funny times and times that made them angry too, talking over fights as well as fun. Then a child can live the death like a story he is part of. There will be fewer dark corners, fewer scary pictures, no muted words he must not understand. And when the story is remembered well, fully felt and finished, a child can go on to turn new pages in his life.

After a while, the sun came out. The children went to the park. Grandpa wasn't there, but they could remember when he was.